GHOSTS
AND
GRAVESTONES
OF
SAVANNAH
GEORGIA

GHOSTS
AND
GRAVESTONES
OF
SAVANNAH
GEORGIA

JOHN F. STAVELY

Historic Tours of America, Inc.
Savannah, Georgia

Library of Congress Control Number: 2006934095

ISBN Number: 9780975269848

First Edition

Author — John F. Stavely

Editor — Dana Ste.Claire

Assistant Editor — Lana Gantner

Publication Design & Production — SGS Design, New Smyrna Beach, Florida

Printing — Tennant Printing Company, DeLand, Florida

All photographs by John F. Stavely

Shadows of the underworld.

ACKNOWLEDGMENTS

*I*t would be nearly impossible to list all of the people who have contributed to this book, but many thanks to everyone who was involved and a very special thanks to Historic Tours of America Inc., Chris Belland and Ed Swift III for developing the creative environment needed to produce this book.

Without the support of the following people this book would not exist:

> Charlie Brazil and the great team at Old Town Trolley Tours® and
> > Ghosts & Gravestones℠ in Savannah
> Ed Swift IV
> The many wonderful ghost tours and people in Savannah
> Kate, Jesse, John, Aaron and Ben
> Everyone else (you know who you are!)

Most of all, my infinite thanks goes to my wonderful wife, Cindy, who tells me when I'm wrong and supports me endlessly. Also, to Carly the Magnificent, who inspires me to live large and be my most creative each day … she always makes me smile.

Seize the moment of excited curiosity on any subject to solve your doubts;
for if you let it pass, the desire may never return,
and you may remain in ignorance.
—William Wirt

A face in stone at Factor's walk.

CONTENTS

Deep into that darkness peering, long I stood there wondering, fearing, doubting, dreaming dreams no mortals ever dared to dream before.

—Edgar Allen Poe,
The Raven

FORWARD

I have always been fascinated with the rich paranormal landscape of Savannah, and I have experienced many eerie things and have heard many persuasive tales there. But it was earlier in my life that my belief in the supernatural took a convincing turn. The events that happened over several weeks in Maryland in 1993 would forever change the way I thought about ghostly experiences. It was made clear to me then that something was happening in the world that defied explanation.

Do you believe in ghosts? Have you ever wondered what exists beyond our normal senses of sight, smell, touch, taste and hearing? Are you curious?

Travel with us on a fascinating journey to the ghosts and gravestones of Savannah, Georgia, a town that has been voted the "most haunted city in America" by the American Institute of Parapsychology.

Debates continue about the nature of hauntings and the origins of ghosts, but most agree that something is happening that transcends the reality we all know. Savannah is one of those ideal places to study the paranormal because you can immerse yourself in the experience.

Founded in 1733 by British General James Oglethorpe, Savannah has a long history of conflict, drama, celebrity and despair. Modern day citizens of this town are gracious yet reserved when they speak of the strange occurrences, ghostly visitations and spectral manifestations that characterize the city. On this paranormal plane, Savannah can seem like an unforgettable dream, even if it is not always acknowledged.

This book explores strange and unusual occurrences that took place over several hundred years in Savannah, Georgia. In some cases, names, locations and circumstances were altered to protect the privacy of the individuals involved, but in every situation the accuracy of what happened and how those present experienced it has been carefully preserved. The rest is for you to decide.

Do you believe?

A quiet moment in the spiritual world.

INTRODUCTION

The boundaries which divide Life from Death are at best shadowy and vague. Who shall say where the one ends, and where the other begins?
—Edgar Allen Poe

*A*s I approached the front desk of the River Street Inn, I immediately sensed that this was no ordinary hotel. The air hung still and thick in the lobby and I felt surrounded by people even though the room was empty. My first instinct was to walk back out the door.

The front desk clerk was cheerful as she checked me in. As I turned to head for my room (with an uneasy feeling) I stopped and asked her, "Any stories of hauntings here?"

She hesitated and looked around to see if anyone else was listening. In a very soft voice she said, "lots of people have strange things happen to them here, but we're not supposed to talk about it." I pressed her for more information and she told me of apparitions guests had seen in their rooms and in the lobby. She pointed out that one of the most "active" spots was the hallway leading to the evening wine and hors d'oeuvre room. Guests also reported sightings and strange occurrences on the original two floors of the hotel. As she told me of seeing a man dressed in antique clothing standing in the lobby one night, a newly arriving guest walked through the front entrance and she stopped talking. I thanked her before going to my room. I couldn't stop thinking about what she said and set out to explore the hotel right away.

The long hallway filled with antiques was inviting and transported me back to an earlier time. As I turned the corner to the elevators, I saw something out of the corner of my eye. I quickly turned my head in this direction and found myself staring at a tall grandfather clock ticking away. Something about the imposing clock drew me in and as I stepped closer, studying the rich wood and swinging pendulum, a reflection flashed over the glass of the clock face. Thinking someone had walked behind me I turned to find that no one was there. The hair on my arms stood up as I pushed the elevator button and quickly made my way to the second floor and the haunted hallway I was told about earlier.

As the doors opened on the elevator, I looked out to find the stone walls of an atrium. They were beautiful walls fashioned out of ballast stone, materials that were carried for balance in the cargo holds of ships long ago. When the hotel was built in 1817, these stones were used for walkways and construction on the riverfront. Now they transported me back to an earlier day when cotton warehouses lined the riverfront and men would yell and heave the cargo from the tall-masted sailing ships. For a moment, I believed I was there, onboard. The haunted hallway demanded my attention and I looked down the long quiet walk with doors on each side and snapped a few photographs to see what might turn up. I made my way down to the end of the hall, taking in the flavor of old Savannah. Everything I had read and heard about the dark, draping atmosphere of this historic town was coming to light and I was eager to seek out more of it.

Open doors beckon.

Where spirits rise.

FROM THE GRAVE

It is the unknown we fear
when we look upon death and darkness, nothing more.
—J. K. Rowling

We'll Never Leave

Men of broader intellect know that there is no sharp
distinction betwixt the real and the unreal...
—H.P. Lovecraft

*F*amed Savannah resident Jim Williams was a successful man by any measure. Antiques were his primary business and he enjoyed the interesting history of objects, people and architecture. Many recognize his name because his life was featured in the book and movie *Midnight in the Garden of Good and Evil.*

It was no surprise to anyone when in 1963 he decided to save and restore two historic homes downtown by relocating them to empty lots he owned on East St. Julian Street. But what should have been a simple procedure became one of the most haunted episodes in Savannah history.

In the garden of evil?

The two historic homes were located on East Bryan Street, just four blocks away from the William's lots. Both mysteriously survived the great fire of 1820 when over four hundred houses in Savannah went up in flames around them. When the movers began to tow the first house, it suddenly and unexpectedly collapsed and a worker was killed. Despite the circumstances and what many believed to be a "bad omen," the second home, the Hampton-Lillibridge House, was moved to its 507 East

Julian Street location and settled into place for restoration.

Soon after, the relocated house began to earn its reputation as the most haunted house in Savannah. As workers started the restoration, they heard strange noises coming from the second floor. Footsteps, scraping and faint voices were heard almost daily and it quickly became a source of entertainment for the workers. Jim Williams would often arrive at the house to

Site of a real exorcism.

inspect the day's work only to find the men standing around listening to the ghostly sounds. The mysterious sounds were convincing enough, but then apparitions began appearing in the upstairs windows. Several witnesses related stories of two men, one dressed in black and the other dressed in gray, materializing in the windows when it was known that no one was in the house. The events became so commonplace and troublesome after Jim Williams moved into the restored house that he sought out help to rid the house of the unwelcome spirits.

On December 7, 1963, the Bishop of the Episcopal Church of Georgia performed a Rite of Exorcism in the Hampton-Lillybridge House. No paranormal events took place in the home for almost ten days following the exorcism, but then they began again. Not long after Jim Williams moved to a different house.

After moving out of the home, Jim Williams relayed a story about an unusual discovery at the lot where the Hampton-Lillybridge House would move. It seems that workers found an old burial crypt in the vacant lot during its preparation. They claimed it was empty, so they filled it in and covered it over before the house was moved right on top of it. Who was buried in the crypt and why was it now empty? Could this be the source of hauntings in the house? We may never know.

LOVE IS ETERNAL

*There was something awesome in the thought of the solitary mortal
standing by the open window and summoning in from the
gloom outside the spirits of the nether world.*
—Sir Arthur Conan Doyle, *Selecting a Ghost*

*A*nna watched hopelessly as the ship sailed east on the river towards
the Atlantic Ocean. The love of her life was on board and he might never
return to her. In her deep sadness, she saw only one way to console
herself – she plunged out of the second story window and landed on the
unyielding bricks below.

Thus begins the tale of the house at the corner of East President and
Lincoln Streets, the 17Hundred90 Inn. The colorful history of the building
that stands here reminds us that not all things are what they first appear
to be. Guests at the historic inn are often visited by a spectral presence
many believe to be Anna herself. Many have reported seeing a young
woman in the
courtyard or in the
upstairs windows
dressed in "antique"
clothing. They
say she looks sad
and upset.

One of the most
convincing pieces of
evidence that Anna
or another ghost
may be present was
a rocking chair
located in what the
innkeepers called
Anna's room. The
chair was seen
many times slowly
rocking back and

Anna's calling.

forth by itself. It was so disturbing that the management removed it from
the room. Unseen footsteps are often heard but the source is never found.
Some have seen windows and doors open and close on their own. Others
have heard a female voice or the jangling of jewelry in an empty room.

Is love eternal? It seems so.

Eternal guardians.

I'm Watching You

A mind once stretched by a new idea never
regains its original dimensions.
—Anonymous

*M*ary Telfair ran her home with stern dignity. When she decided to convert it into one of the first art museums in the South, her policy was firm: "no eating, smoking, drinking or gambling" were the rules that everyone was expected to follow, even after she died in 1875.

The imposing figures of famous artists stare down at you in front of the Telfair Museum. If you stare at them long enough, you would swear that they move from time to time. Science explains this phenomenon as a trick of the mind and eye but many are not so sure given the haunted history of this building.

One of the most vivid and famous paranormal incidents occurred in the parlor where Mary Telfair's portrait hung, a painting that had been there for as long as anyone can remember.

The museum staff wanted to rearrange the room but as they attempted to remove the portrait, a large chunk of the rotunda ceiling collapsed, barely missing them. So they kept the portrait where it was.

Unexplained winds blow through this house and many have seen movement from the

Follow the rules...

corner of their eye or have heard footsteps where none should be.

To this day, parties are still held outside of the main house because of unusual incidents that chased guests outside when they attempted to break Mrs. Telfair's strict social rules. Few dare to eat, drink, smoke or gamble within the walls of the home. And if you happen to pass by on a warm sunny day, stop and stare at the statues for a while… if you are brave enough!

25

Dark rooms harbor dark secrets.

MURDER AND MAYHEM

On the outskirts of every agony sits some observant fellow who points.
—Virginia Woolf

On December 10, 1909 a brutal murder took place in a boarding house that stood just across from the Visitors Center. The deadly arsenal of an axe, knife and hammer were used to end the lives of three women in a most horrific way. As you can imagine, the people of Savannah were outraged at this violent act and citizens armed themselves to search for the vicious killer. Soon after, a man was taken into custody and arrested for stealing tools after police noticed blood on his clothes and under his fingernails. The man, Bingham Bryant, declared his innocence but the police were certain they had their criminal. They had only to obtain a confession from him, but he continued to deny his guilt with great conviction. In an attempt to coax a confession out of Bryant, the police recreated the murder scene in great detail at the very spot where the crime was committed using mannequins and gallons of red ink. The police led Bryant into the awful crime scene, sure that this would cause him to break down and confess, but he did not.

Suddenly a ghostly figure appeared and pointed at Bryant, accusing him of the terrible crime. Bryant smiled at the makeshift ghost and calmly said, "You are mistaken." The policeman portraying the "ghost" took the sheet off his head when he realized that his ploy would not force a confession. With no further interrogation, they released

Old cobweb in the corner.

Bingham Bryant and, as it turned out, the real killer was the husband of one of the victims and he was sent to prison for life.

The boarding house was soon haunted with ghostly noises and voices. When bloodstains were found oozing through the walls, the owners tore down the cursed house. But horrible events have a way of lingering around, and to this very day the new building that stands in the place of the original boarding house is filled with cries and screams and sometimes oozing walls. It seems that the past is not willing to be forgotten.

Shadowy stroll.

Shadows in the Night

The oldest and strongest emotion of mankind is fear, and the oldest and strongest kind of fear is fear of the unknown.
—H.P. Lovecraft

The legend persists of a boy giant named Renee Rondalia who locals say lived in the 1700s in a section of town known as "Foley's Alley," near East Broad Street. Stories describe a young boy who towered over boys and girls of his age. The other children taunted and teased him because he was different. Renee kept to himself, but the townspeople whispered rumors of odd behavior, including cruelty to small animals. When a little girl was found strangled, all eyes turned towards the home of Renee Rondalia. The furious crowd marched to the door of his house and pounded until his parents slowly opened it to shouts of "hand him over!" His parents pleaded his innocence and the townspeople finally agreed to place Renee under house arrest to avoid any further trouble until they could sort out the truth. Then tragedy struck again - another child was found strangled and, although Renee was confined to his home, everyone believed he was guilty. He was quickly bound and led through the streets of Savannah to a hangman's noose the mob had hastily prepared. The jeers and taunts of the angry crowd were the last sounds Renee Rondalia heard before the rope pulled tight around his neck and strangled the life from him.

But the humiliation did not end there.

A marsh was Renee's final resting place.

Strange figures walk in the still of the night.

The townspeople agreed that such a terrible person could not be buried in the cemetery alongside respectable citizens and a makeshift pit was dug in the marsh near the river where Renee's giant, lifeless body was dumped unceremoniously. Perhaps this final insult was what caused the hauntings, who can say? But soon doors were barred and shutters nailed shut as the townspeople began to see a huge hulking figure wandering in the night. Children knew if they misbehaved or stayed out too late, this giant apparition might find them and exact his revenge. The legend of Renee Rondalia grew over the years and the facts have been blurred along the way. But if you happen to be walking the streets after midnight and hear heavy footsteps or see a giant shadow on the wall...be afraid!

DANNY'S BED

There are mysteries which men can only guess at,
which age by age they may solve only in part
—Bram Stoker, *Dracula*

There are some Savannah residents who believe they have connected with the afterlife. One famous story involves an antique bed purchased by the Cobb family for their teenaged son. According to the parents, strange things started to happen right after the bed was set up in their son's room. He began to feel uncomfortable in the room as if someone was watching him, breathing cold air down his neck as he lay in the bed. Soon objects began to move around the room as if someone was trying to make a point. Several times, the son discovered family photos on his nightstand turned face down. More disturbingly, when he would return upstairs from breakfast to find several items placed in the middle of the bed as though someone had been playing with them.

Determined to find out the source of the very convincing haunting, Mr. Cobb tried to make contact with the spirit by posing questions. According to Mr. Cobb, he asked for the name and age of whoever had moved the objects and left paper and crayons in the room for fifteen minutes in hopes of a response. To the family's astonishment, they returned to find "Danny, 7" in big block letters on the paper. More writings would follow adding to the mystery of who had owned the bed and why he was still connected to it. The family continued to explore the supernatural until the experiment took an ugly turn. Objects began to break and after a wall hanging flew across the room just missing the son – perhaps a ghostly temper tantrum - the bed was removed and "Danny" seemingly went with it. No other

Do you see him?

Spectral winds.

paranormal incidents happened after the bed was taken out. Members of the Cobb family moved on with their lives, but each still wonders who Danny was and in whose house he resides today.

Can objects hold spiritual energy? There is wide belief that they can. In Victorian times, mirrors were covered after someone died to prevent spirits from being trapped in the glass. Folklore suggests that objects often become "possessed" by good and evil spirits. Does this have some basis in fact?

If you happen to be browsing through an antique shop and find an old bed that peaks your interest or a table that would look great in your kitchen, make sure to ask about the history of the piece. You just never know.

HAUNTED HOUSES

The limits of the possible can only be defined by
going beyond them into the impossible.
—Arthur C. Clarke

The Davenport House

Fear is a slinking cat I find Beneath the lilacs of my mind.
—Sophie Tunnel

Isaiah Davenport, master builder from Rhode Island, constructed a house at 324 East State Street in 1820, but was only able to enjoy living there for seven years before he fell victim to yellow fever. At the time, his wife Sarah was eight months pregnant with her tenth child. Three children had died in infancy, which was common at that time, so she and the seven children remained in the house until 1840. The William Baynard family of Hilton Head, South Carolina, occupied the house for the next half century. After the Baynards moved out, the building was divided up and rented as apartments until 1955 when Katherine Summerlin, owner of the Goette Funeral Home (opposite the Kehoe House), purchased the property. She in turn resold it to the Savannah Historic Trust where it was restored as a museum. The home ignited the Trust's campaign to restore Savannah's historic homes.

Nearly two hundred years of drama, emotion and history fill this house. Today, the ghost of a young Victorian girl is often seen upstairs. No one is sure who she is but she seems to know her way around the house. The fourth floor is now off limits to visitors, but on the three floors below, visitors have claimed to see a transparent yellow cat walking through the house that always disappears when approached.

A ghostly cat roams the halls of Davenport.

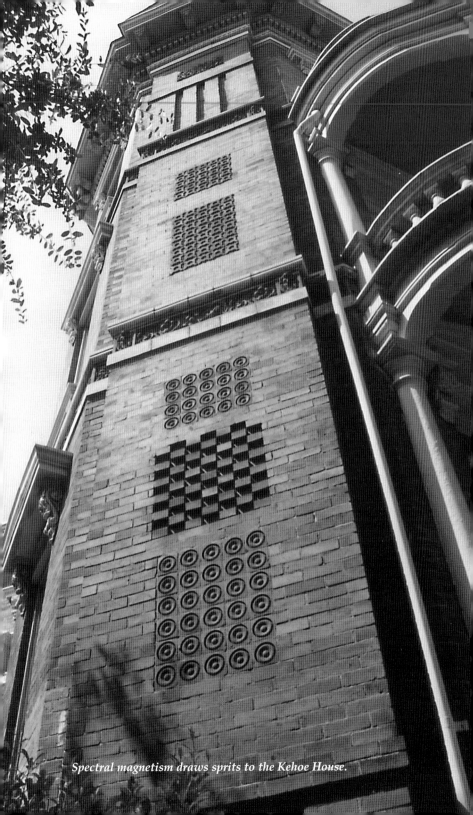

Spectral magnetism draws sprits to the Kehoe House.

KEHOE HOUSE

Then away out in the woods I heard that kind of a sound that a ghost makes when it wants to tell about something that's on its mind and can't make itself understood, and so can't rest easy in its grave, and has to go about that way every night grieving.

—Mark Twain, *The Adventures of Huckleberry Finn*

The elaborate Kehoe house at 123 Habersham Street holds many secrets. It is said that the building has a certain spectral magnetism for hauntings. All of the trim and features on and around the outside of the house traditionally would be made of wood or concrete, but Mr. Kehoe

owned the local iron works and naturally used cast iron to adorn his house. Today, the ornate iron can be seen as everything painted white.

The home was built in 1892 for Mr. And Mrs. Kehoe, their ten children and many grandchildren. Until 1963, it was a funeral home with embalming and preparation in the basement and viewings on the second floor. Such a place can stir the imagination.

Today guests hear "things" that go bump in the night and see apparitions sitting in chairs or gliding through the house. Music from an unknown source is often heard but never found. Some guests

Things go bump in the night at the old funeral home.

have heard the sound of their name being called softly in the night. If you are feeling adventurous, take a room there and see what happens.

Guests from the past still come for dinner at the Owens-Thomas House.

OWENS-THOMAS HOUSE

I will die here where I have walked.
And I will walk here, though I am in my grave.
I will walk here until the pride of this house is humbled.

—Charles Dickens

The Owens-Thomas house, built by William Jay at 124 Abercorn Street, is renowned for its beauty and history. The Marquis de Lafayette himself addressed the citizens of Savannah in 1825 from the balcony of this house. It has known power and prominence and it seems that the former residents cannot bear to depart from this.

In the dining room of this historic house museum, the table is neatly arranged as it might have appeared in the past. When the staff arrives to open in the morning, they often find chairs pushed back and table settings askew as though some phantom figure had dined there the night before. Dogs grow concerned and hover about the front door whimpering. You never feel alone as you explore the rooms of the house; the strange chill that rolls up the back of your spine as you walk through is testament to its haunted nature. Apparitions of both men and women frequently materialize in the rooms and hallways. It seems the beauty of the house is only surpassed by its haunted reputation.

Even the dogs are wary.

41

HAMILTON-TURNER HOUSE

Be wary then; best safety lies in fear.
—Shakespeare, *Hamlet*

In 1873, William Pugh Hamilton built the Hamilton-Turner house at 330 Abercorn Street. Hamilton was one of the town's most prominent citizens and this was one of the finest homes ever built in the city. As was the custom of the day, his six children spent most of their time out of sight on the top floor with their nanny. Mr. Hamilton provided them with diversion and amusement up there; even a pool table was installed to pass the time. Still the children felt isolated and would purposely make loud noises and drop things on the floor when their parents had guests over just to get a reaction. After the house was converted into apartments a century later, the new owner started to hear the faint sound of children's voices drifting down from the upstairs rooms. They would call out, "mama" or "papa." Sometimes a loud thump or the sharp crack of pool balls would startle the people living downstairs. One day, an orange billiard ball bounced down the stairs, landing on each step, finally rolling to the feet of a woman working in the gift shop. It seems that the Hamilton children are still trying to get our attention.

Where phantom billiard balls bounce down century old stairways.

43

Till death do us part... or bring us together.

Juliette Gordon Lowe House

All meanings, we know, depend on the key of interpretation.
—George Eliot

*J*uliette Gordon was born on Halloween, October 31st, 1860, in the dead of night. She would carry this magical mark with her for the rest of her life. Gordon grew up at a time when spiritualism, séances and communing with the afterlife were popular, and it was no surprise that she would go on to found the Girl Scouts of America where tales around the campfire are still a tradition.

House of apparitions.

Apparitions and odd happenings occur frequently in the house at 142 Bull Street. Immediately following the death of Juliette's mother, Nellie, in 1917, her sister in law, Margaret, was startled by the ghost of General Willie Gordon, Nellie's husband, who had passed away five years before in 1912. He appeared in all of his ghostly glory at the exact moment of his wife's death and Margaret watched him slowly walk out of the bedroom and down the staircase. As she breathlessly told everyone what she had just seen, the family butler appeared, crying. He had just seen the very same ghost of General Gordon coming down the stairs and going out the front door. If you need proof that love conquers all, you need look no further: the afterlife was a long-awaited reunion for Willie and Nellie and a new journey for the couple.

A mysteriously cracked mirror greets guests in the parlor.

SORREL-WEED HOUSE

Nay, fly to altars; there they'll talk you dead;
For fools rush in where angels fear to tread.
—Alexander Pope, *An Essay on Criticism*

*W*alking into the basement of the Sorrel-Weed House, you immediately understand why so many ghost-hunting teams have sought out the house to document paranormal activity. By the time you reach the parlor, where a huge cracked mirror stares down into the room, your senses are tingling and the air is thick with ghostly energy.

This was the very first house to be built on Madison Square in 1840. It also happens to be the site of the second bloodiest battle in the American Revolution, the Siege of Savannah fought in 1779. The house was built for Francis Sorrel and his second wife, Matilda. The Antebellum mansion was one of the most well known social centers in town and it hosted many grand parties that lasted late into the night. The Sorrels raised eight children here too, so the house was always bustling with family activity over the years. Then tragedy struck.

On a spring day in May of 1860, Matilda Sorrel climbed the stairs of the servant's quarters to discover her husband in the arms of the lead servant, Molly. Stunned and betrayed, Matilda fled the room crying. She raced to the main house, ran up the stairs to the master bedroom, threw herself over the second story balcony, and plunged to her death in the courtyard below. Just two weeks later, the servant Molly was discovered hanged, and to this day no one knows if she took her own life or if she was murdered. The guilt ridden Francis Sorrel never remarried and the house was never the same.

Today, the owners are awakened to strange sounds in the middle of the night. Music and laughter echo through the halls at odd times, voices murmur and occasionally faces appear in a mirror or window only to disappear just as quickly as they materialized.

The spot where Matilda landed in the courtyard has an odd, thick feel to it and photographs have revealed strange orbs and mists. It is common for the ghost hunter's infrared equipment to reveal children's handprints on the wall in the basement.

Objects randomly move in the house. The once placid dwelling today seems to be a restless place that has a weighty effect on the emotions of those who come into the house. Visitors report a range of unexplained feelings from great joy to heaviness and profound sadness. Some are so moved that they have to leave the house.

Perhaps Matilda and Molly are still roaming the halls of the Sorrel-Weed House, remembering the joyous parties that were tragically cut short one dark day in 1860.

A thin line separates the dead.

WHAT LIES BENEATH YOUR FEET

*Sometimes the world of the living gets mixed up
with the world of the dead.*
—The Others

Is Olgethorpe's mystical design reason for Savannah's hauntings?

THE SQUARES

An evening wind uprose too, and the slighter branches cracked and rattled as they moved, in skeleton dances, to its moaning music.
—Charles Dickens, *Martin Chuzzlewit*

General James Oglethorpe, founder of the British colony of Savannah and son of a knight, dated his family lineage back to the mighty Saxon Kings. It is rumored that he practiced ancient mystical rituals common to the Templar Knights and Freemasons during the 18th century. Oglethorpe's original town plan of Savannah was designed to be exactly 1,000 cubits on each side. Some claim that this original design serves to trap spirit energy within the city limits and intensify its hauntings.

The squares have been gathering places for the citizens of Savannah for centuries. Is it any wonder that they might gather here after their passing too? Of all the places in town, the squares are the most compelling for the paranormal folks. You can hardly walk through the parks during the day or the night without feeling like you are being watched or that something spiritual is nearby. Many have reported that if you stand in the squares when all is quiet, you can hear voices from the past murmuring about past town events. A sudden gust of cold wind may leave you breathless. The air is often filled with a strong sweet scent, the smell of the past. Yes, my friends, the town is thick with spiritual energy!

Bring Out Your Dead

What was it? They could not tell themselves. They only knew that the black shadows at the top of the staircase had thickened, had coalesced, had taken a definite, batlike shape.

—Sir Arthur Conan Doyle, *The Land of Mist*

The town's Public burying ground was originally established near Wright Square and was closed in 1750 when the Colonial Cemetery was opened. Although the town relocated the early gravestones to the new cemetery, they left behind the bodies that were buried under them! These lost skeletons often and inconveniently pop up during construction in the area of the original cemetery. And even more eerie, as trees grow and push up through the soil they collect bones that are sometimes found hanging from their branches. This has led to the Savannah folk expression that "the trees have teeth" in the city.

The old Lindsay & Morgan Company building where the Public burying ground once was located is occupied on the first and second floors, but the third and fourth floors remain empty. Former tenants reported disturbing noises on a regular basis. One night, a tenant heard for several hours the noises of furniture moving around. The next day he mentioned it to the shopkeeper who explained that neither he nor anyone else had been in the building that night. Something else had been busy rearranging the offices. Former tenants on the third and fourth floors also heard footsteps downstairs that came up the stairs and stopped just outside their doors. After

Gravestones move, the dead remain.

53

several frightening occurrences, they waited for the footsteps to arrive again, pushed the door open to surprise the intruder, but only found an empty hallway. The police were called, but they too found no evidence of a trespasser.

Immediately in back of the building is the old York Lane Theatre that was forced to move its operations because of many strange events that occurred there. Actors would hear ghostly voices and footsteps while they performed, sometimes causing them to stop in mid-performance on stage to listen. When the actors and theater staff started to see apparitions during productions, everyone quickly moved out. Today, much of the building is still empty, a darkness that continues to invite spirits from the ground below.

Burying grounds of Savannah.

COLONIAL PARK CEMETERY

Fear is the main source of superstition,
and one of the main sources of cruelty.
—Bertrand Russell, *An Outline of Intellectual Rubbish*

*T*he "newer" c. 1750 Colonial Park cemetery has had its share of maintenance problems, too. Here, hundreds of graves were desecrated over the years by well-meaning town folk, grave robbers, and scavenger animals. Of the over 10,000 graves originally plotted at Colonial Park, less than 600 markers remain. So where are the rest? Just look under your feet! Former town planners felt that the cemetery looked too crowded, so they "reduced" it by removing every other stone and placing them on a far wall. But they once again left the bodies behind, so as you are observing a surviving gravestone, you are likely standing on top of an unmarked grave. The old stones can still be seen along the southern (?) wall.

As you explore the cemetery, look for the ornate subterranean vaults and crypts scattered throughout. The "half moons" in front of many of the vaults are actually entranceways to subterranean chambers. Over time, leaves and soil have filled in the stairwells leading down into the ground and below these layers of age-old humus are steps that will take you to the vault door. Beyond the door to the vault is where bodies were laid to rest. Here they rested peacefully until General William Tecumseh Sherman came to the town during the Civil War. The winter of 1864 was

Restless spirits have been separated from their graves.

bitter cold and Sherman's soldiers camping on the grounds of the cemetery broke into the vaults to stay warm. They unceremoniously dumped the dearly departed outside and the soldiers slept where the dead had rested the night before. To amuse themselves, the soldiers changed the dates on many of the gravestones. With an added numeral one reads, Miss Susannah Gray: struck down by lightning at the age of 121 years! While it is true that she was struck and killed by lightning, she was only 21 years of age when it happened. The stone further reads that virtue and modesty were her adornments.

There are many tragic stories that characterize the centuries-old cemetery. In the center is an area reserved for duelists who perished while defending their honor. Famous author James Wilde who died in such a fight in 1815 at the age of twenty-three is buried here. His epitaph reads: *He fell by the hand of a man who, a short time before, would have been friendless but for him.* Poor James. He was shot through the heart on the fourth exchange. His brother composed an unfinished poem in his remembrance. My favorite lines read:

*My life is like the summer rose,
That opens to the morning sky;
And ere the shades of evening close,
Is scattered on the ground to die.*

Stark reminders of age-old death.

WRIGHT SQUARE

You said I killed you - haunt me, then! The murdered do haunt their
murderers, I believe. I know that ghosts have wandered on earth.
Be with me always - take any form - drive me mad!
Only do not leave me in this abyss, where I cannot find you!
—Emily Bronte

In early Savannah, many colonists were sent to the gallows to pay for their crimes. They were often hanged in the town squares to warn lawbreakers that criminal ways would always come with severe consequences. Even women paid the awful price. Soon after the colony was settled in the 1730s, a young indentured servant named Alice Riley kept house for a heartless, cold-blooded master. Every morning she would wash his long flowing white hair as part of her duties. She hated this man and washing his hair each day grew increasingly unbearable, so one day she and her husband decided to hold his head under the water and drown him.

The couple ran for their lives after murdering the master, but they were soon captured and Alice was sentenced to death and ordered to the gallows. In her plea, Alice revealed that she was with child. Not wanting to hang a pregnant woman, the town officials waited for enough time to pass to determine if she was telling the truth or just stalling for time. She was indeed with child and after his birth several months later the sentence was carried out. Alice was hanged high in the trees for all to see and her child was put up for adoption. They say that Spanish moss will not grow well on the trees in the section of Wright Square where Alice was hanged because her spirit keeps plucking it off. You will notice, however, that Spanish moss grows freely in the opposite corner. Why you may ask? It is the area where her husband was hanged and now he rests in peace.

Spanish moss drapes the thick Savannah air.

Tomochichi's final meeting place... or is it?

I'll Be Back

It's no accident that the church and the graveyard stand side by side.
The city of the dead sleeps encircled by the city of the living.
—Diane Frolov and Andrew Schneider

*I*n Wright Square you will find a large stone in its southeastern corner. If the sunlight is just right toward the end of the day, you will notice shadows dancing across this rock like the shadows on a cave wall created by firelight.

In 1739, a Native American named Tomochichi was buried in Wright Square. He was the Yamacraw Indian chief who allowed James Oglethorpe and the first Georgia colonists to settle on Yamacraw Bluff in 1733, where the original town of Savannah was settled. Tomochichi's help was key to the success of the colony during its first few difficult years. Over time, the Chief and Oglethorpe became close friends and they even journeyed together across the Atlantic to visit the royal court in England. After his death, Tomochichi was buried in a place of honor in the square. Over the years, the town forgot that the chief was buried in the Square, and in the 1880s his grave was dug up to make way for the construction of a monument to William Washington Gordon, founder of the Georgia Railroad.

What should have been the final resting place for an important figure in Savannah history was unknowingly destroyed and desecrated that day. Later, the mistake was discovered and in 1899, on the 160th anniversary of Tomochichi's death, the large rock monument was dedicated to what many consider to be the "co-founder" of Savannah. Most townsfolk believed that all was made right with the Yamacraw chief, but others were unsure. After all, his body is not under the rock. Could the restless spirit of Chief Tomochichi still be haunting Wright Square? There is proof that he is.

Local legend says that if you walk around the monument three times and ask, "Tomochichi, Tomochichi, Where Are You?" and then put your ear to the rock, you will hear the chief reply, "Nowhere." Others claim that if you walk around the monument backwards and ask, "Tomochichi, Tomochichi, What are you?" and put your ear to the rock, he will humbly reply, "Nobody."

Every nook and cranny holds a secret.

NOOKS AND CRANNIES

One need not be a chamber to be haunted; One need not be a house;
The brain has corridors surpassing material place.
—Emily Dickinson

YO HO HO AND A BOTTLE OF RUM

*Man cannot discover new oceans unless he has the
courage to lose sight of the shore.*
—Andre Gide

For anyone that has read "Treasure Island" by Robert Louis Stevenson, the lure of the sea is undeniable. Many say Stevenson's book was inspired by the Pirate House located on East Broad Street in Savannah. Perhaps the most interesting feature on the Pirate House grounds is the "Shanghai" kidnapping tunnels that run underground from the house to the river below. The brick cellar still exists and the management is pleased to show guests the location of these now sealed passageways. It is said that many unfortunate young men were "recruited" for seafaring duty by pirates, rendered unconscious by the strike of a club and quickly whisked away through the tunnels in the dark of night. When they awakened on board the ship, it would be too late - they were doomed to a life of hard work on the high seas.

The Pirate House is one of many places in Savannah that is filled with dramatic tales of high adventure. Adding to the lure of the Pirate House is the colorful history of the ground on which it was built. The site rests on part of the original "Trustees Garden" founded in 1733 to experiment with plants and crops that might grow in the new British colony. Steeped in lore and legend, it is thick with sounds and active apparitions. Echoing through the night are songs of the sea and wails of young men dragged off long ago to serve the pirate's ship. Close your eyes for a moment and the slap of the canvas sails will brush your ears, the smell of the salty sea will fill your nose. And if you are lucky, you may even come face-to-face with a bearded, cutlass-carrying pirate doomed to wander this place for all eternity.

MOON RIVER BREWING COMPANY

Fear is nature's warning signal to get busy.
—Henry C. Link

*W*alk into this busy brewpub at 21 West Bay Street and you will hardly notice the age of the building. Most customers never see the unfinished upper floors that are reserved for employees and group meetings. Here, echoes of the past are well known.

When the building was the City Hotel in the early 1800s, the landmark hosted thousands of travelers with southern hospitality and charm. The bar was a popular spot for the influential citizens of Savannah to meet and talk about the affairs of the day. Sometimes, a heated discussion would lead to insult and a duel of honor. Many gentlemen crossed over the Savannah River to South Carolina to settle their differences, but rarely did all of them come back. Today it seems that the spirited debates are manifested as seldom debated spirits. Customers and employees believed that the high emotion and drama that once took place in the Brewing Company pub is the reason for the many supernatural sightings and encounters that characterize the building.

Many have reported seeing, hearing and smelling unusual phenomenon in the pub. Some occurrences are more convincing than others, like the fully formed apparitions, sometimes seen gliding from room to room. One waitress walked into the stockroom to discover a woman standing at the back of the room in a green antique dress. The server watched in horror as the ghostly presence vanished in front of her eyes and she quickly ran out of the room. Another employee was taking inventory when he felt uneasy, as if he was being watched. He anxiously glanced around but saw nothing. Suddenly, he smelled the distinct odor of sweet perfume and felt a hand touch his shoulder. In haste, he stumbled out of the room and refused to go back upstairs that day. Creaking floorboards, cold spots and unseen voices fill this historic building and paranormal investigators flock to it by the dozens to witness the spiritual theatre.

This former hotel is still busy with paranormal guests.

67

SHRIMP FACTORY

By the pricking of my thumbs, something wicked this way comes . . .
—William Shakespeare, *Macbeth*

*L*ike most historic buildings along the Savannah River, the Shrimp Factory a century ago served as a cotton warehouse, bustling with commercial activity. Imagine as you look around the dozens of full-sailed schooners and tall ships lining the riverfront delivering their goods, men yelling and heaving their heavy bales of cotton high in the air. Cotton made Savannah prosperous beyond belief but over the years, this wealth and activity faded and soon the warehouses sat empty, crumbling and alone. Here in the abandoned holds and back alleys, restless spirits wait for the return of the living.

The Shrimp Factory on East River Street has its own resident spirits. Upstairs in the building is a small forgotten room where the sounds of moaning are often heard. The moans start out low as soft cries and grow in intensity, as if you are listening to someone or something in pain. Employees refuse to go into this room alone and who can blame them? Some have said that in winter the terrible moaning gets louder and more disturbing as though someone is calling out from beyond the grave. We may never know what spirit resides upstairs, but rest assured, they are unlikely to leave anytime soon.

The shrimp factory serves up spirits of many kinds.

Spiritual Savannah lies temporarily quiet in the morning light.

Sleep Tight

Everything that happens happens as it should, and if you observe
carefully, you will find this to be so
—Marcus Aurelius

*S*avannah visitors often have supernatural encounters but wish to remain anonymous. Here is one recent incident involving a family that experienced the supernatural firsthand at a downtown hotel. The story was relayed to the hotel staff at check out.

The night before, the father of the family woke up about three in the morning and noticed the bathroom door was wide open after he had closed it. A quick check revealed his wife and two children sound asleep but he sensed that something just wasn't right. His mind began to play tricks on him as he looked at the darkened shapes around the room, some of which seemed to move out of the corner of his eye. As he lay there in the bed deciding what to do next, he suddenly heard a loud, clear female voice sigh directly behind him! Startled, he sat up and turned around, but saw nothing. Did the voice come from an open window? No, it was very close as if someone was standing right next to him. He lay back down and once again heard a woman sigh loudly. His heart pounding, the man got out of bed and walked around the room trying to figure out what was happening. He closed the bathroom door, walked back to bed and finally fell asleep. In the morning, the bathroom door was wide open again and he assumed that someone had opened it during the night as he slept.

When the family went to the front desk the next morning, the father asked about the number of ghost tours in the area. The woman behind the counter must have misunderstood, thinking he has asked about the number of ghosts in the hotel and nervously replied, "We have three." The man said, "In the square?" where he had seen the tours starting. "No," she said, "right here in the hotel. We have a ghost soldier, a cat and a little girl." A chill ran up the man's neck as she continued, "just this morning a guest complained about all the furniture we were moving in the room above him, but there is just storeroom above his room and only our maintenance staff goes in there and we know that no furniture was being moved when he heard it."

The man realized that the sighs he had heard the night before were not from a woman but from a little girl. It all made sense and he shared his experience with the woman behind the desk. "The events seem to come and go in streaks," she told him and said that he was not the first to report hearing a sigh. "Was your bathroom door open when you woke up this morning?" she asked. The ghostly pattern was well documented.

If these walls could talk.

Who Goes There?

We are born, we live, we die among supernatural
—Napoleon Bonaparte

*J*ust outside the city limits, standing guard over the Savannah River is the imposing Fort Pulaski. When it was constructed, beginning in 1829, it was considered to be the most advanced fortification of its time, but by the time it was finished eighteen years later, the brick fort was considered old technology and vulnerable to new weapons and military attack. This was most evident in 1862 when the local militia inside the fort was pounded into submission by Federal gun batteries set up on Tybee Island. Colonel Olmstead and his men surrendered the fort and there was great shame brought on from losing the battle. Perhaps the high emotion and lingering memories of this skirmish and other battles surrounding Fort Pulaski keep the spirits of former soldiers forever bound.

Sightings of ghosts in soldier uniform are common here and the air is thick with paranormal expectations when you visit. Not long ago, historic re-enactors in a film production had an encounter they will never forget. It was during the making of the movie *Glory* that a group of nine actors visited the fort on the way to the filming. As they walked around the outside walls several of them noticed a young man in a Confederate lieutenant's uniform who was not part of their group. They gave him a nod of greeting. He shouted, "Halt!" in a mild Savannah accent. "Don't you men salute a superior officer when you see one?" he asked them as he took a step closer. The re-enactors looked at one another in confusion, shrugged, and a couple of them threw a quick salute. As the group

walked away, one grumbled, "Who does he think he is?" The Confederate overheard the man and reacted abruptly, "Sir, I don't know to what you are referring and frankly I don't care! Your insolence, however, will be noted and not tolerated. Now fall in! Colonel Olmstead has recalled all work parties. The Yankee attack is imminent!"

The re-enactors saw that visitors in the Fort were watching and they decided to play along. They formed up into a line and waited for the next order. "Attention!" the Lieutenant bellowed and the group straightened up. "About face!" he yelled and the group turned around and waited for the order to march. They waited and waited. Nothing happened and finally when they looked behind them, the Confederate lieutenant had disappeared into thin air!

Then re-enactors searched the Fort grounds for the young man in Confederate uniform, as well as the movie set nearby for the duration of the filming, but the officer was never seen again. Their only explanation was that an officer from the past had stepped forward in time to order his men to safety. If you visit Fort Pulaski and see a young Lieutenant approaching, it might be in your best interest to come to attention and give him a salute … just in case.

Still... she waves.

When Will You Return?

Because I could not stop for Death, he kindly stopped for me,
the carriage held but just ourselves, and immortality.
—Emily Dickinson

*O*n the riverfront stands the statue of a young woman named Florence Martus who once lived with her brother on Elba Island at the mouth of the Savannah River. In 1887, a series of events occurred that would change her life forever and earn her the name, the "Waving Girl."

In the later 19th century, life on Elba Island was isolated and nearby Fort Pulaski seemed exciting to Florence. She began to give tours of the fort to visitors. During one of these tours, young Florence met a handsome Navy Lieutenant who swept her off her feet. It was love at first sight for the both of them. They spent all of their time together until the day came for her new love to resume duty and sail off on his ship. He promised to return as soon as possible to marry her and gave her his white Navy neckerchief as a token of his undying love. With tears rolling down her face, Florence waved at the departing ship and stood in the same spot gazing off in the distance for hours after the ship had disappeared from sight.

Months passed with no word from her beau. Florence watched every ship day and night in hopes that he was on it. Soon she began to wave the neckerchief at every ship in case someone on board knew her Lieutenant. Word quickly spread about a young girl that waved at ships on the Savannah River and used a lantern by night while her trusty collie lay at her feet. Sailors far and wide knew about Florence and her lost love.

Florence's devotion endured for 44 years until her death in 1943. The townspeople were so moved by her vigil that they erected a statue in her honor. Some say she never stopped waving. Sailors still report seeing the ghost of Florence waving a white cloth or a lantern. As they get closer, she fades away. It seems her loyalty to the sailor who never returned is never ending. If there is ever such a thing as an honorary Savannah ghost, it should be Florence.

THE SMELL OF DESPAIR

It began in mystery, and it will end in mystery,
but what a savage and beautiful country lies between.
—Diane Ackerman

Charred remains of old Savannah.

Raging Fire

I saw her, in the fire, but now. I hear her in music, in the wind, in the dead
stillness of the night," returned the haunted man.
—Charles Dickens, *The Haunted Man*

$\mathcal{F}$ire can appear alive if you watch it long enough. It can devastate and renew. Some believe that spontaneous fire is a sure sign of ghostly activity and Savannah has had its share of destruction through fire. The first major fire destroyed over 300 homes in 1796, structures that at the time comprised most of the city. 1820 was a difficult year, too, with the yellow fever claiming thousands of victims followed by another major fire. Conditions were dry and in only eight hours over 500 structures were lost in the inferno. The catastrophe, considered one of the worst fires in American history, left Savannah unrecognizable. In 1865, a huge blaze leveled over 200 homes, but 1889 might have been the worst. The roaring flames once again devastated the densely populated town and hundreds of houses were left smoldering by the time the fire was brought under control. Many thought the whole town would be incinerated and disappear. Witnesses claim that the 1889 fire danced and roared as though alive. Savannah has rebuilt on the ashes of destruction so many times that one has to wonder what unseen role the spirits play in tragedy.

Victims of pestilence.

YELLOW FEVER

It is required of every man, the ghost returned, that the spirit within him
should walk abroad among his fellow-men, and travel far and wide; and,
if that spirit goes not forth in life, it is condemned to do so after death.
—Charles Dickens, *A Christmas Carol*

The "Yellow Jack," as yellow fever was referred to in earlier times, would claim thousands of lives in Savannah throughout her history. Unknown at the time, mosquitoes were the culprit behind the fever. Port cities were the most affected when the mosquitoes would travel by ship to new areas. Many citizens simply moved farther inland rather than face the yellow menace.

The disease was frightening to early Savannah citizens because of its unknown cause and sudden, devastating effects. It begins with high fever, muscle aches and headache, followed by vomiting. The eyes begin to turn red as the skin turns yellow. Blood oozes out as hemorrhages, and seizures and delirium torment the victim. Family and friends can only stand by and watch helplessly as the symptoms compound and cause death. It must have been frightening to witness such a violent and mysterious demise of a family member or friend. Some say that the violent deaths account for the great unrest in those claimed by the yellow fever, just one more reason why Savannah has so much para-normal activity.

History layered at Laurel Grove Cemetary.

Do you dare pass through?

STRANGE WAYS

All truth passes through three stages.
First, it is ridiculed.
Second, it is violently opposed.
Third, it is accepted as being self-evident.
—Arthur Schopenhauer

An eerie glow beyond the trees.

Buried Alive!

A fool without fear is sometimes wiser than an angel with fear.
—Lady Nancy Astor, *My Two Countries*

During the Victorian times, "spiritualism" came into fashion as many believed that the living could communicate with the dead. Séances, mediums and stage shows sprang up to satisfy the public's hunger for proof of an afterlife and spirit activity of deceased friends and relatives. Many of these "supernatural" demonstrations were nothing more than elaborate magical hoaxes using special effects and assistants. Perhaps that was why they still feared the grave.

Few things terrified the Victorian public more than being buried alive. Accidental burials in the 1800s were often the result of limited understanding of comas and high fevers where victims would appear to be lifeless and were quickly buried by mistake. Coffins exhumed later would show signs of violent struggles such as fingernail marks on the insides of the coffin lids where the "deceased" tried to claw their way out. To remedy this

Fingernails scrape the inside lids.

situation, axes, hammers and pry bars were often placed inside the casket with the dearly departed in the event they should awaken underground and have the strength to dig themselves out. Many thought this was impractical and began installing small tubes from the coffin to the surface where a rope was connected to the deceased's hand at one end and to a bell at the top at the other. Men would be hired for the specific purpose to listen for the bells and quickly dig up the undead. This is where the term dead ringers comes from. There is no evidence that this system ever worked, but it must have been an interesting graveyard shift for the bell tenders. Imagine in the middle of the night hearing a bell ring from the graveyard!

Beware of ominous crows perching.

HOODOO

He who is afraid of a thing gives it power over him.
—Moorish Proverb

*I*n Savannah and the surrounding "Low Country", the practice of Hoodoo is well known to locals. Root doctors and conjurers are feared and respected for their ability to dole out good or bad luck, improve health, or even bring the dead back to life.

The simple definition of Hoodoo is the practice of and belief in African-American folk magic. American Indian and European folkways also played a part as the African practices were assimilated into New World cultures. Some folks call it "rootwork" or "conjuration" since it often involves herb remedies, incantations and casting of spells. It is not to be confused with Voodoo which has a different origin and is practiced by very few compared to Hoodoo. The essence of Hoodoo is the belief that these rituals will affect your life in a positive or negative way. That is the power it holds.

Hoodoo is difficult to find in Savannah today. If you need a "mojo bag" or "goofer dust" to cast a spell, where do you go? A scene from *Midnight in the Garden of Good and Evil* shows a Hoodoo ritual performed in Savannah, leading one to believe that Hoodoo practitioners are common in the city. But trying to find a root doctor requires knowing someone who knows someone. This quality adds to the mystery. But make no mistake, the belief is strong and the magical practices are woven into Savannah's supernatural landscape. So if you open your front door and see white powder sprinkled on the stoop, don't step over it! A Hoodoo doctor has "laid a trick" on you and you had best beware.

A bad sign.

ENDINGS

Fear is a question: What are you afraid of, and why?
Just as the seed of health is in illness, because illness contains information,
your fears are a treasure house of self-knowledge if you explore them.

—Marilyn Ferguson

*S*avannah truly is a town that is *built on its dead*. Over three hundred years of history have shaped and colored the local scene. War, fire, plague, pirates and time have given life to and enhanced the stories and legends that characterize this historic place. The city's charm is compelling, and I am drawn here again and again.

This town is like no other. No matter how often I walk the streets and squares of Savannah, I can't help looking over my shoulder or feeling a presence nearby. Maybe it's the way the light filters down through the historic houses and age-old trees. Or maybe it's the thickness of the air or the eerie feeling I get when I realize that I might be walking over an ancient and forgotten burial site. Savannah will always be one of my favorite places to look for the odd, the unusual and the paranormal. If you can't find it here… I'm certain that you won't find it anywhere.

Happy hunting!

Old Savannah lingers on and on.

ABOUT THE AUTHOR

*J*ohn Stavely is the National Director for Historic Entertainment for Historic Tours of America, Inc. He develops performance programs for HTA attractions, museums, Ghosts & Gravestones tours, and various history and entertainment-based tours including scripting, costuming, props, evaluation and actor training. His first book in this series, *Ghosts and Gravestones in St. Augustine, Florida* (2005), is the most popular and sought-after ghost tour book in the city and is currently in its third printing.

John Stavely in Savannah.

Stavely's lifelong interest in the paranormal has led him to many interesting places and people in the country. He continues to document and share through programs and publications his supernatural experiences in historic cities across the country. His television appearances include the *Discovery Channel, Travel Channel, History Channel* and *The Food Network*. He has been featured on several nationally televised shows including *Ghost Hunters, Most Haunted Places, Great Hotels,* and the *Best Of* series.

A living history "heritage actor" by specialty, Stavely is considered one of the most accomplished first-person historic character performers in the country. His British Colonial period Jesse Fish character is well known and critically acclaimed. His repertoire includes a 19th century Henry Flagler, an 1800s traveling snake oil salesman named Dr. Dewey Cheetum, and an 18th century pirate, Captain John Kent. He lives in St. Augustine with his wife, Cindy, and daughter, Carly. A former Golf Professional and PGA administrator, John Stavely now devotes a fulltime career to historic entertainment.

Ghosts and Gravestones of Savannah
is a haunted adventure aboard the **Trolley of the Doomed**

Join us for dark tales and visit some of the most haunted
buildings in town with your ghost host

For more information please visit
www.historictours.com or call **912-233-0083**

For your next visit to St. Augustine,
take along a copy of John Stavely's
Ghosts & Gravestones in St. Augustine...

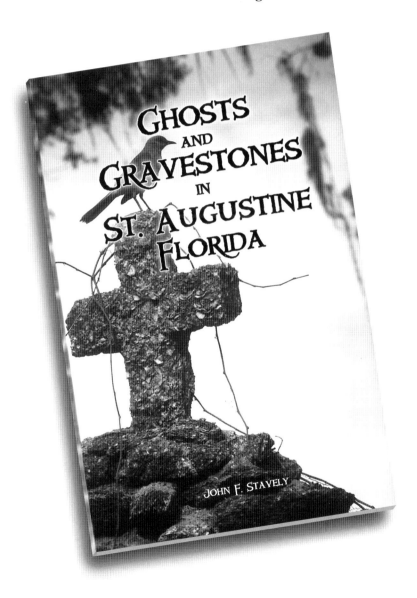

What is really eerie about this book is John Stavely's uncanny
ability to capture through his camera the paranormal
things he describes. The black and white photographs
are moving, and sometimes disturbing, and really
make the book. It's pretty convincing that he has
some sort of supernatural perspective
on the world and Savannah.
—Nelson Norwood, Parapsychologist

Ghosts & Gravestones is the perfect
companion for ghosthunters in
Savannah and for anyone taking a
ghost tour. John Stavely's ghost tour
book is the most popular here.
—Diane Lane, Ancient City Tours

Creepy! This book is the "Best Of" list of Savannah's spooki-
est places! It's fun touring the city with this book in hand and
reading about the "behind the scenes" stories of historic sites.
—Lon Gantner, American Ghosthunter

Historic Tours
of America, Inc.
234 MLK Boulevard
Savannah, Georgia

ISBN 0975269844

329448
BK GHOST & GS SAV

90000

9848

$7.99

P9-AHD-614